Derby

Illustrated Guide to the County with c

Text by Pat Ashworth
Photography by Frank Fell

Dry stone walling, near Eyam

Contents

1

Introduction

Travellers eager to experience the rich variety of English landscape and heritage can find it in microcosm in Derbyshire. A journey from the four compass points of this endlessly surprising county takes in exhilarating wilderness, dramatic gorges, gentle dales and craggy moorlands. It embraces winding rivers and still waters, great country estates and towering relics of industry. There is living, breathing history in the market towns, villages and hamlets, where a deep love for the countryside keeps old traditions alive.

Everyone has a different perspective on Derbyshire, from the
parascender soaring above the Eastern Edges to the explorer descending
into the caverns of Castleton. The county has no coastline and yet is an
island of tranquillity in the surrounding sea of big cities. It is a place of
spiritual solace and escape. 'There are things in Derbyshire as noble as
in Greece or Switzerland,' pronounced Lord Byron, expressing as only a
poet can perhaps, the influence and inspiration of the place.

Hope Valley, near Castleton.

The Dark Peak

Admiration is tinged with respect for the magnificent Dark Peak in the north of the Peak District National Park. It can be liberating and elating or bleak and hostile for the walker on the great millstone grit plateau of Kinder Scout (636m) and Bleaklow (633m), where crossing the groughs of the peat bogs can be like negotiating a glacier. This is one of the toughest sections of the Pennine Way, which starts from Edale with the steep ascent of Jacob's Ladder. Its wild beauty is characterised by the cotton grass that bobs like fibre optics among the bilberry and heather, and the eerie croak of red grouse on a damp and misty day.

The names are graphic and evocative: Rushup Edge, the Grindsbrook Skyline, Black Hill, Snake Pass. On the Great Ridge, south of Kinder, stands Mam Tor, an iron age hillfort with history and attitude, accessible on a flagstoned path. The stern and

watching ruin of Peveril Castle commands the spectacular gorge of Winnats Pass in the Castleton area, where visitors can penetrate the mile-long Peak Cavern with its 30m high Great Cave; glide by boat to the 'bottomless pit' of Speedwell and marvel at the mineralogy of Treak Cliff.

The Howden, Derwent and Ladybower reservoirs with their impressive dams and forested slopes give the landscape of the Upper Derwent Valley an openness and expansiveness that has been likened to the Canadian lakes in miniature. History is literally just below the surface here, with the remnants of submerged villages visible in a dry summer from the surrounding ridges.

1 *The Devil's Elbow*
Serendipity… the vista from a quiet, winding road above Longdendale, north of Glossop.

2 A Boundary Marker for the Peak District National Park

This magnificent park extends to an area of 542 square miles and is the most visited National Park after Mount Fuji.

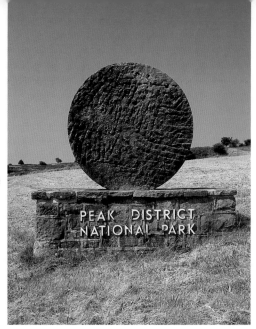

3 Glossop

No factory smoke rises now from Glossop, a pleasant valley town which had 56 mills working at the peak of its manufacturing activity. Its history can be seen at the Heritage Centre.

4 Alport Valley and Alport Moor

A view little changed over the centuries. There are no roads here, the river meanders through unhindered and the dramatic landslip of the Alport Castles still commands attention.

5 *Undulating moorland with sweeping views*
*Millstone grit gives the Dark Peak its name, but it is alight
with bright green slopes and springy purple heather.*

⑦ Howden Reservoir

*A circuit of the two upper reservoirs,
Howden and Derwent, has been
described by the writer, Mark
Richards, as 'probably the gentlest
and most rewarding of walks that
the High Peak can offer the
non-committed walker'.*

6 *Ladybower Reservoir*
*Autumn tinges the slopes of the
Ladybower Reservoir and the
Derwent Valley. The west tower of
the Derwent Dam holds the
memorial to the 617 squadron,
immortalised in the 1954
Dambusters film starring
Richard Todd as Wing
Commander Guy Gibson.*

8 *Dam walls and towers of
Howden Reservoir*
*Completed in 1912, the Howden Reservoir
was the first of the great Derwent Valley
reservoirs to be built.*

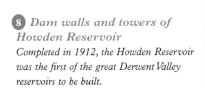

9 Lose Hill and the Vale of Edale

The River Noe threads its way through the gentle, pastoral landscape of the Vale of Edale, with a scattering of villages and hamlets bearing the names of the five ancient farming communities known as 'booths'. Edale is the access point to Kinder and the start of the Pennine way.

10 The Great Ridge

This is one of the most exhilarating walks in the Peak, a striding path that takes in Lose Hill Pike, Mam Tor (the 'shivering mountain') and Win Hill and offers glorious views over the Hope Valley.

11 The Old Nag's Head, Edale

The village of Edale is the starting point for the hardest stretch of the 256-mile Pennine Way, accessed by the steep and twisting flight of steps that is Jacob's Ladder.

12 Kinderscout
*Sunlight falls on the slopes
below the Kinder plateau
and spreads to the reservoir
beyond - a landscape that
has many moods and never
ceases to thrill.*

13 Winnats Pass
*The old road to
Castleton from the west
snakes through this
spectacular limestone
gorge, a dry valley that
was at the heart of the
17th century lead
mining industry.*

14 *Peveril Castle*
This awesome and uncompromising remnant of the power of the Norman kings was built by William de Peverel in the 11th century and watches unblinking over Cave Dale.

15 *'The Stork'*
The old lead mine of Treak Cliff Cavern boasts some wondrous stalagmites and stalactites, and is still worked for its rich veins of Blue John.

16 *Speedwell Cavern*
Speedwell Cavern has the thrill and mystery of being only accessible by boat via a flooded tunnel underground.

The Eastern Edges

The great boulders and crags of Baslow, Curbar, Froggatt, Stanage and Derwent Edges, are a playground for walkers and climbers and an adventure paradise for children. Here, as though on top of the world, you hear the clink of harnesses and the slither of ropes on stone as hands and helmets appear with suddenness from the rock face below. The views are magnificent, with a scattering of abandoned millstones making dramatic centrepieces for artists and photographers. Higger Tor, the enigmatic hilltop fortress of Carl Wark, the Longshaw estate and the ancient oak woodland of Padley Gorge are favourite places on and around these Eastern Edges.

From Curbar Edge, the distant jet of water from Paxton's Emperor Fountain visible on a fine day is a reminder of the proximity of Chatsworth, ancestral home of the Dukes of Devonshire. The House, parkland, woodland, garden and riverside make up a glorious pastoral landscape. Neighbouring great houses include Hardwick Hall, the mighty Elizabethan testament to the flamboyance and ambition of Bess of Hardwick, and the stunningly restored Bolsover Castle with its medieval pretension and fantasy.

Smaller in scale but as brimful of history is Eyam Hall, in a village full of poignant reminders of the Great Plague and the now legendary heroism of the vicar and villagers in containing it. A church tall enough and grand enough to be a cathedral dominates the village of Tideswell and is a legacy of the prosperous 14th century wool industry, whilst the church in much-visited Hathersage can boast the grave of Little John, legendary henchman to Robin Hood. Chesterfield is the largest town in the county, as famous for its open-air market - one of the largest in the country - as for the crooked spire of the Church of St Mary and All Saints.

17 View from Bamford Edge
Looking down on the world from Bamford Edge, with the gentle slopes of Offerton Moor and Shatton Moor rising on the far side of the valley.

18 Bamford Edge
Curious rock formations have evolved over the years in many parts of the Peak District.

19 Bamford Edge
Shale and sandstone
created these proud and
mighty pillars.

20 Millstones at Stanage Edge
Abandoned quern-stones give the impression of having
rolled into place and simply rested where they lay.
The Edges were quarried for the stones, used for milling corn.

21 The Cathedral of the Peak
The eight pinnacles of Tideswell Church,
a soaring Perpendicular building dating
from the 14th century, are a visible
landmark for miles around.

㉒ *Padley Gorge*

Generations of boots have trodden the steep, mossy, boulder-strewn path above the tumbling Burbage Brook, flanked by oak trees and populated by wood warblers and pied flycatchers in spring.

㉓ *Carl Wark*

In the foreground, the remains of a boulder wall ten feet high and a turfed rampart that would have defended this ancient hilltop fort on Hathersage Moor.

㉔ *Higger Tor from Carl Wark*

The path leading up from Carl Wark to Higger Tor, the high point of a favourite circular walk from the Longshaw Lodge Visitor Centre.

25 *Eyam Hall and village stocks.* The Black Death decimated the population of Eyam, as the parish registers show, but the building of Eyam Hall in 1671 is living proof that the village recovered and life went on.

27 *Chatsworth House and the River Derwent*
The glory that is Chatsworth, bathed in golden sunshine.
The ancestral home of the Dukes of Devonshire is magnificent: a treasure house of classic and contemporary works of art that led the Dowager Duchess to observe: 'We live in furnished rooms. There are a great many of them, and they are very well furnished'.

26 *Fallow deer at Chatsworth*
The parkland is as beloved as the House itself.

28 *Edensor village*
The Sixth Duke of Devonshire had the estate village removed out of sight of the House in 1830. Eccentric architecture with Swiss, Italian and Gothic influences gives it an almost film-set feel in the pastoral landscape.

30 **Country House at Baslow**
The autumnal shades of the Virginia Creeper give added warmth and colour to this beautiful house.

29 **Baslow Cottage**
Thatched cottages overlooking Bar Brook, on a riverside path in Baslow village leading into Chatsworth Park.

31 *Chesterfield Market and Market Hall*
Derbyshire's biggest town can boast more than 250 stalls in its colourful market, flanked by the beautifully refurbished 19th century Market Hall.

32 *Knifesmithgate, Chesterfield*
The narrow streets and inns around the Market Place in Chesterfield town centre are a vivid reminder of its medieval past.

33 *The Crooked Spire, Chesterfield*
They say the devil sneezed and that's why the spire on the Church of St Mary and All Saints leans 287cms from its true centre. Whatever the scientific explanation, the curiosity of the spire has put the town on the map.

34 Bolsover Castle

Built not for war but simply to impress King Charles I and Queen Henrietta on a one-day visit in 1634, Bolsover Castle towers above the Vale of Scarsdale and has been stunningly restored by English Heritage.

35 Mock battles in a mock-medieval castle

Musketeers re-enact early battles, though Bolsover was built for pleasure and has been called 'a temple of love'.

36 Poppy fields near Eckington

37 Hardwick Hall

Built in 1597 by Bess of Hardwick, and now in the care of the National Trust, breathtaking Hardwick is renowned for being 'more glass than wall' and is famous for its tapestries and textiles.

The Wye Valley

The River Wye meanders south-easterly through lovely Chee Dale, Millers Dale, Cressbrook and Monsal Dale at the heart of the Peak District, joining the Derwent at Rowsley to flow down to Matlock and Cromford. Few can resist Haddon Hall, the 14th century seat of the Duke of Rutland, where to step through the wicket gate into the paved courtyard and medieval manor house is to encounter the past without any inducement on its part or effort on the visitor's.

Bakewell has all the attractions of a thriving market town, with local foods to sample and a fascinating mix of architectural styles to ponder. The three-arched packhorse bridge and the limestone cottages that line the village street at Ashford-in-the-Water

38 *Monsal Dale Weir*
The River Wye winds its leisurely course over millraces and weirs and through some of the loveliest and most tranquil scenery in the Peak.

are an inspiration for painters. The fairy lights and illuminations of Matlock Bath give the spa town something of a seaside feel down below. Up above, cable cars sway high over the Derwent Gorge to point travellers to the little Switzerland that is the Heights of Abraham. Further south, at Cromford, Derbyshire's proud industrial heritage is highly visible in the commanding presence of Arkwright's Mill, the Cromford canal and the remains of the Cromford and High Peak Railway. Over to the west, Wirksworth's lead-mining and quarrying past is commemorated in the National Stone Centre, whilst Crich is home to the National Tramway Museum.

39 Chee Dale
This lovely valley,
with its riverside walk,
stepping stones and
dramatic buttresses, is a
canyon in miniature.

40 Monsal Dale Viaduct
A sweeping view of the Wye Valley
from Monsal Dale Head. The
railway line carved its way through
the hills to carry trains to Manchester,
and this much-photographed piece of
track was amongst the most
spectacular in England.

41 Millers Dale
Ash trees trail their
delicate branches into
the waters of the Wye,
beneath the limestone
gorge of Millers Dale.

42 *Water-cum-Jolly Dale*
Great cliffs and still waters lift the heart in this
well-loved dale, the site of a 19th century cotton mill.

43 *Sheepwash Bridge, Ashford-in-the-Water*
Time stands still at Ashford-in-the-Water, where sheep were penned in a stone fold by this
three-arched packhorse bridge before being made to swim across the river to clean their fleeces.

44 Bakewell

The spire of the parish church of All Saints dominates lively, busy, bustling Bakewell, an historic market town with wide appeal.

45 Bakewell Bridge

Graceful willows overhang the river by the five-arched Bakewell Bridge, built in 1300 and one of the oldest bridges in England.

46 The famous Bakewell Tart

In Bakewell itself, they call it a Pudding… just one of the many local foods to be enjoyed in Derbyshire.

47 Haddon Hall

A majestic fortified manor house, much of it dating from the 14th and 15th centuries. Closed up for two centuries, its long hibernation preserved all the medieval and Tudor features and makes it a favourite location for film-makers.

48 *Hall Leys Park, Matlock*
Boating on the lake is one of the great pleasures in a town that has always welcomed visitors.

49 *Matlock Dale*
Whitewashed houses perch on the steep sides of the gorge on the approach to Matlock Bath, fashionable as a Spa town from the 17th century onwards.

50 *North Parade, Matlock Bath*
Shops and restaurants add to the many attractions of Matlock Bath.

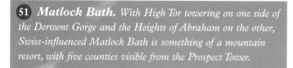

51 *Matlock Bath.* *With High Tor towering on one side of the Derwent Gorge and the Heights of Abraham on the other, Swiss-influenced Matlock Bath is something of a mountain resort, with five counties visible from the Prospect Tower.*

52 *Matlock Illuminations*
Fairy lights strung out along the riverbank, and decorated boats on the water lend annual enchantment at Matlock Illuminations.

53 *Wirksworth Church.* St Mary's Church is famous for its stone carvings, in a town that was a lead mining and quarrying centre and which now boasts the National Stone Centre. Much of George Eliot's novel, *Adam Bede*, was set around Wirksworth.

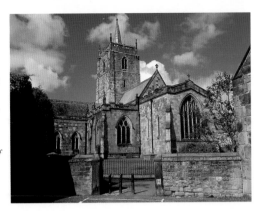

54 *Masson Mills, Matlock Bath*

This historically important and very imposing mill was established in 1783 by Richard Arkwright, the 'father of the factory system'. It is regarded as the finest surviving example of an Arkwright mill and now houses a working textiles museum, a heritage centre and a Shopping Village within the mill complex.

55 *Cromford Mill.* Cromford Mill has a special place in history as the world's first successful water-powered cotton mill, built by Richard Arkwright in 1771. The five-storey mill complex was the first factory of its kind and used innovative technology invented by Arkwright. It is a much-loved Derbyshire building, under restoration by the Arkwright Society since 1979 and featured on BBC Television's 'Restoration' programme, where it scored highly. The mill stands at the start of a 15-mile World Heritage Site that includes Masson Mills and stretches along the Derwent Valley to the Silk Mill in Derby.

56 **Lea Wood Pumphouse, Cromford**

The Cromford canal carried raw cotton, coal, lead, iron, limestone and gritstone. A once vital link in the chain of industrial waterways, it now gives pleasure to strollers along the towpath to High Peak Junction.

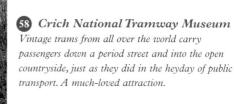

57 **Cromford**

The village is claimed to be the world's first purpose-built village for factory workers, in the valley that was the cradle of the industrial revolution.

58 **Crich National Tramway Museum**

Vintage trams from all over the world carry passengers down a period street and into the open countryside, just as they did in the heyday of public transport. A much-loved attraction.

59 **Crich Memorial Stand**

A lighthouse in a sea of land and a wash of sky; a beacon with tower views across eight counties. The Stand, built in 1921 on the site of previous beacon towers, is a monument to the men of the Sherwood Foresters regiment killed in two world wars.

The White Peak

Limestone is white and bright, a scenery harmonised by green fields, complemented by clear water and made both orderly and disorderly by drystone walls. The dales of the White Peak - which stretches roughly from Buxton in the west to Matlock in the east, and from Castleton in the north to Thorpe in the south - are less formidable than the Dark Peak but no less elating. Best known of all is Dovedale, where the craggy ravine evolves into Milldale, Wolfscote Dale, and Beresford Dale before reaching Hartington with its white ducks on a mere-like village pond. Lathkill Dale is a secret valley, a lost world inaccessible by car, tumbling with water and scattered with wild flowers. The Manifold Valley is commanded by Thor's Cave, just over the border into Staffordshire.

Cyclists, walkers and horseriders can cover distances on the High Peak Trail and the Tissington Trail, with the villages of Monyash and Youlgreave over to the east. All six of Tissington's wells are 'dressed' on Ascension Day with exquisite pictures

made from flowers, ferns, mosses, leaves and bark, in thanksgiving ceremonies replicated throughout many of the villages of Derbyshire. Tissington Hall, home of the FitzHerbert family since Tudor times, is another attraction here.

There are curiosities too in the landscape of the White Peak: remnants of coral reefs in the distinctive conical peaks of Chrome Hill and Parkhouse Hill at the northern end; evocative ruins like the Magpie Mine at Sheldon; the prehistoric sites of Arbor Low and the Nine Ladies Circle on Stanton Moor. Ashbourne, a Georgian town close to the southern gateway to the White Peak, boasts the famous melée that is the Shrovetide Football Game, played annually over the two days of Shrove Tuesday and Ash Wednesday, on a three-mile pitch in the streets and surrounding areas.

60 Lathkill Dale
*Clear, sparkling and wildlife-sustaining,
the broad and beautiful River Lathkill.*

61 Thorpe Cloud, Dovedale
A 'clud' in Old English was a rock, and the ascent to
the summit of this mini-mountain makes Thorpe Cloud
(287m) a first peak for many an aspiring climber.

62 The Stepping Stones at Dovedale
A famous beauty spot, where more family photographs
get taken than anywhere in the Peak. Easy riverside
walking takes the visitor up to Milldale, through
stunning woodland dominated by awesome craggy pillars.

63 Beresford Dale

Izaak Walton and Charles Cotton, the occupant of Beresford Hall, perfected the art of fishing in a retreat here on the quiet upper reaches of the Dove. Walton published his 'Compleat Angler' in 1653.

64 Wolfscote Dale

Out of leafy Beresford Dale and into open meadowland… the contrast is startling and the scenery of jagged limestone outcrops and screes spectacular.

33

65 *Youlgreave*

Anyone born and brought up in pretty Youlgreave (also known as Youlgrave) is entitled to call themselves a Pommie - the name said to derive from the sounding 'pom pom' brass of the Youlgrave Silver Band.

66 *Hartington village*

The Perpendicular tower of St Giles Church is a landmark at the heart of a beautiful and compact village with a duckpond, a Tudor manor house (now a youth hostel), and welcome tea-rooms at the end of walks in Dovedale.

67 *Alport village*

The River Lathkill flows through the village of Alport, the starting-point for a five-mile walk to Monyash.

68 *Bonsall*
The market cross at Bonsall, a village tucked away beneath Masson Hill and once home to cotton workers from the mills at Cromford and Via Gellia.

69 *Bradbourne*
A Saxon cross from around 800AD stands in the churchyard at Bradbourne, where the square Norman tower is a fine sight.

70 *Carsington Water*
Sailing, windsurfing, walking, cycling, horse-riding and nature watching... exhilarating activities on the water and around the reservoir, opened in 1992.

35

71 *Tissington Hall.* Home to the FitzHerbert family for 500 years, the ornate Hall with its mullioned windows was built by Francis FitzHerbert in the reign of James I. Paintings by Reynolds, Rubens and Velasquez are among the family treasures it contains.

72 *Tissington well-dressings.* The custom of dressing wells with Biblical pictures dates back to thanksgivings for pure water through the years of the Black Death. It was revived in Tissington in 1615 when the wells did not run dry, despite a drought, and the ceremony takes place on Ascension Day each year.

73 *Tissington Village.* A painter's dream, an English idyll with stone cottages, village green and duckpond. The 13-mile Tissington Trail starts at Parsley Hay and ends at Ashbourne. It is on the trackbed of the old railway and can be accessed from the site of the old Tissington Station.

74 Ashbourne

The 'Oakbourne' of Adam Bede is a lively Georgian market town of cobbled alleys and coaching inns, merchants' houses and market stalls. It boasts a Tudor grammar school and the longest inn sign in England on St John's Street, overseen by a cheery black head.

75 Ashbourne Church

George Eliot called St Oswald's, with its soaring spire, 'the finest mere parish church in England'.

76 Osmaston Village

Brick-built thatched cottages characterise the estate village built to serve Osmaston Manor, home of the industrialist, Francis Wright, whose family owned Butterley Ironworks. Osmaston Manor is now demolished, but the magnificent parkland containing several lakes still remains.

77 Mapleton Church

The octagonal dome of the 18th century parish church of St Mary is a landmark in the peaceful village of Mapleton in the Dove Valley.

37

The Western Ridge

The luxuriant landscape of the Goyt Valley with its blue reservoir, purple moorland and richly wooded slopes, yields to the windswept isolation of Cat and Fiddle Moor (boasting the highest inn in England) and the bleak expanse of Axe Edge Moor before the Western Ridge leaves Derbyshire at Three Shires Head and becomes Morridge in Staffordshire.

Buxton is the principal town of the western side of the county. It is no coincidence

79 *Goyt River and bridge*
The Goyt rises on the slopes of Cat and Fiddle Moor. Picnic sites abound on the shores of the reservoir and by the river as it winds through the thickly wooded valley.

that it resembles Bath in the honey-coloured stone and in
the elegant curve of St Ann's Crescent, which was built
to rival the Royal Crescent of the famous Avon Spa town.
The visitor can take the waters by drawing from
St Ann's Well, be entertained in Edwardian opulence at
the restored Opera House and enjoy the Pavilion and
Gardens amongst numerous other attractions.

78 *Fernilee Reservoir
in the Goyt Valley*
*A shimmering, breathtaking vista
on the rise out of Whaley Bridge.*

80 *The Cat and Fiddle*
The inn has a commanding location, close to the village of Flash and, at 462.7 metres, said to be the highest pub in England.

81 *Three Shires Head*
The packhorse bridge at Three Shires Head, where Derbyshire meets Cheshire and Staffordshire. Local villains exploited the fact that local police had jurisdiction only in their own counties, holding illegal fights up here and counterfeiting money.

82 *Axe Edge*
The wide expanse of Axe Edge Moor.

83 *Buxton Opera House*
*An opulent, sumptuously restored
Edwardian opera house, famous for its
summer music festivals, which began
in 1903. Designed and built by Frank
Matcham, it seats 946 and has a
stage large enough for grand opera.*

84 *The Crescent, Buxton*
The Fifth Duke of Devonshire commissioned the Crescent with its impressive 42 pilasters and 378 windows. Buxton's Great Stable evolved into the Devonshire Hospital and has found a new incarnation as the University of Derby's Buxton campus.

85 *The Pavilion Gardens, Buxton. This ornate bandstand is in the Pavilion Gardens, opened in 1871. The grounds extend to 23 acres of gardens, lakes and recreational facilities, together with play areas for children including paddling pools and a miniature railway. The Pavilion itself contains the grand domed Concert Hall and other rooms, used for conferences, exhibitions and collectors' fairs.*

South Derbyshire
and the City of Derby

The southern end of the county is a reminder that the sum of Derbyshire is more than the parts that are the Peak. Stately homes and country houses abound here too - imposing, 17th century Sudbury Hall; glorious 18th century Kedleston Hall; the time capsule of Calke Abbey (1703), whose treasures lay undisturbed for decades. There are gems too in Melbourne Hall with its fine gardens, and the Gothic-style Elvaston Castle and country park with its fragrant box hedges and elaborate follies.

The 18th and 19th century mills and industrial landscape of the Derwent Valley share with the Great Barrier Reef, the Grand Canyon and a further 750 endangered sites worldwide the inscription of World Heritage Site.

86 *Elvaston Castle*
The grounds and avenues are the glory at Elvaston Castle, remodelled in 1817 with Gothick flights of fancy and now at the centre of a beautiful country park.

The valley saw the birth of the factory system, and the 15-mile heritage site extends from The Silk Mill - Derby's Museum of Industry and History, to Masson Mills at Matlock Bath.

As for Derby itself, it is a university and cathedral city rediscovering its past and imaginatively building its future. The English Romantic painter, Joseph Wright, is one of the city's famous sons, and Rolls Royce one of its most famous manufacturing companies. The Royal Crown Derby Visitor Centre is a principal attraction and the city has become equally well known for its clubs and its vibrant night life. A fitting climax to a Derbyshire tour.

86

87 *Sudbury Hall*

The National Trust owns Sudbury Hall, a late 17th century house with sumptuous interiors that include wood carvings by Grinling Gibbons and painted murals and ceilings by Louis Laguerre.

88 *Kedleston Hall*

Kedleston is in essence one great gallery, a showplace for the treasures and works of art collected by the Curzon family, who completed the Hall in 1765. Now owned by the National Trust, it has magnificent state rooms, and is acknowledged to be the most complete and least altered of any Adam interior.

89 *Calke Abbey*

A baroque mansion completed for Sir John Harpur in 1704, Calke stands in a secluded hollow at the heart of extensive parkland with fine walks. The house is a time capsule, with its contents deliberately left by the National Trust as they were when the house was closed up in the 1920s.

90 *Melbourne pool, church and hall.* *Tranquillity in the gardens at Melbourne Hall, home to Lord and Lady Ralph Kerr and open annually to the public in August. The ornamental pool is a favourite haunt of visitors, and the nearby Church of St Michael with St Mary is deemed to be one of the finest examples of a Norman parish church.*

91 *Repton School*
There has been a school on the site since 1557, and Repton is proud to boast that people have passed through this arch since the 12th century.

92 *The market cross at Repton*
Christianity in the Midlands is said to have first been preached at this spot. Kings of Mercia are buried in St Wystan's church, which dates from around 750 AD.

93 *Netherseal*
The picturesque village centre with its 17th century almshouses is now a conservation area.

94 Trent Lock
Messing about on the river…
Trent Lock is a popular
sailing and boating centre.

95 The Wharf at Shardlow
Once an inland port on the important
Midlands canal and river network,
Shardlow has some fine canal warehouses
and is now a mecca for leisure boaters.

96 The River Derwent
at Derby. *Illuminated at*
night, St Mary's Weir is a
dramatic sight. The waterfront
is at the heart of development
in the city.